GRAPH PAPER MASTERS

DALE SEYMOUR PUBLICATIONS

PARSIPPANY, NEW JERSEY

IMPORTANT NOTE: The grids in this book were computer-created with a high degree of accuracy, but in some cases the printing reproduction process may have introduced a slight margin of error. Additionally, most photocopy machines will cause a minor distortion in one or both directions. For this reason, we do not recommend the use of copy-machine graph paper for any situation in which dimensional accuracy is critical. We believe, however, that you will find these masters suitable for most classroom purposes. For minimal distortion, hold the book as flat as possible against the copier, or carefully remove the desired master from the book before copying.

Dale Seymour Publications
An imprint of Pearson Learning
299 Jefferson Road, P.O. Box 480
Parsippany, New Jersey 07054-0480
www.pearsonlearning.com
1-800-321-3106

Cover design: Rachel Gage

ISBN 0-86651-490-2

15 16 17 18 19 20-MA-05 04 03 02 01 00

Dale
Seymour
Publications

CONTENTS

STANDARD
MEASURE
GRIDS

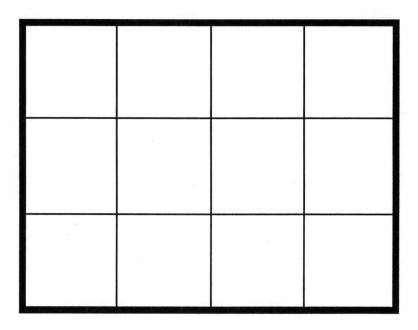

GRAPH PAPER MASTERS · Copyright © by Dale Seymour Publications

GRAPH PAPER MASTERS • Copyright © by Dale Seymour Publications

• GRAPH PAPER MASTERS **5**

GRAPH PAPER MASTERS · Copyright © by Dale Seymour Publications

• GRAPH PAPER MASTERS 7

GRAPH PAPER MASTERS • Copyright © by Dale Seymour Publications

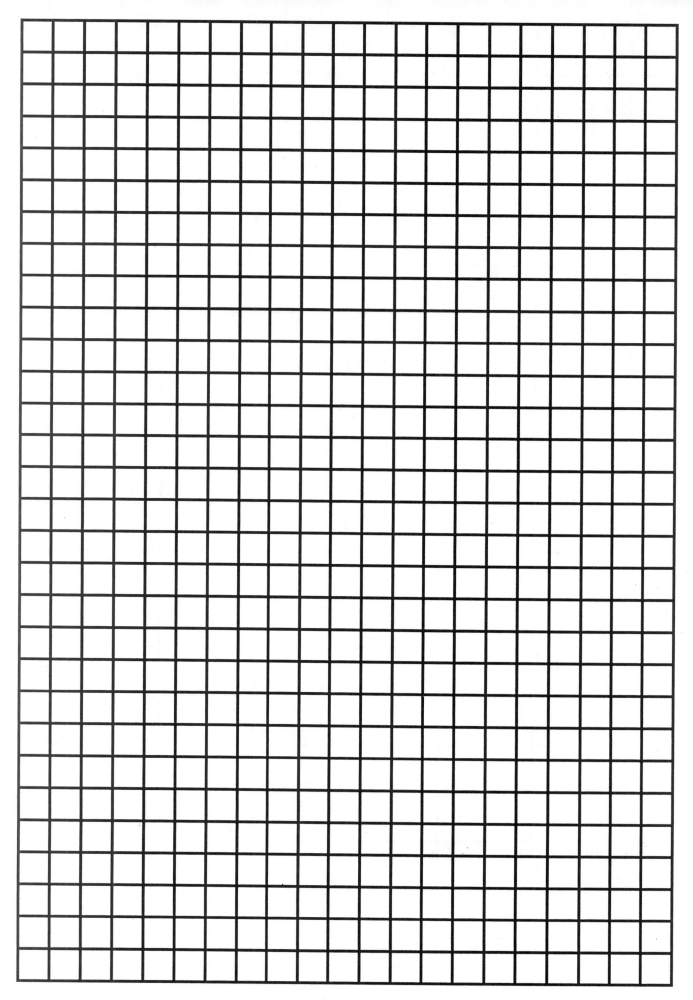

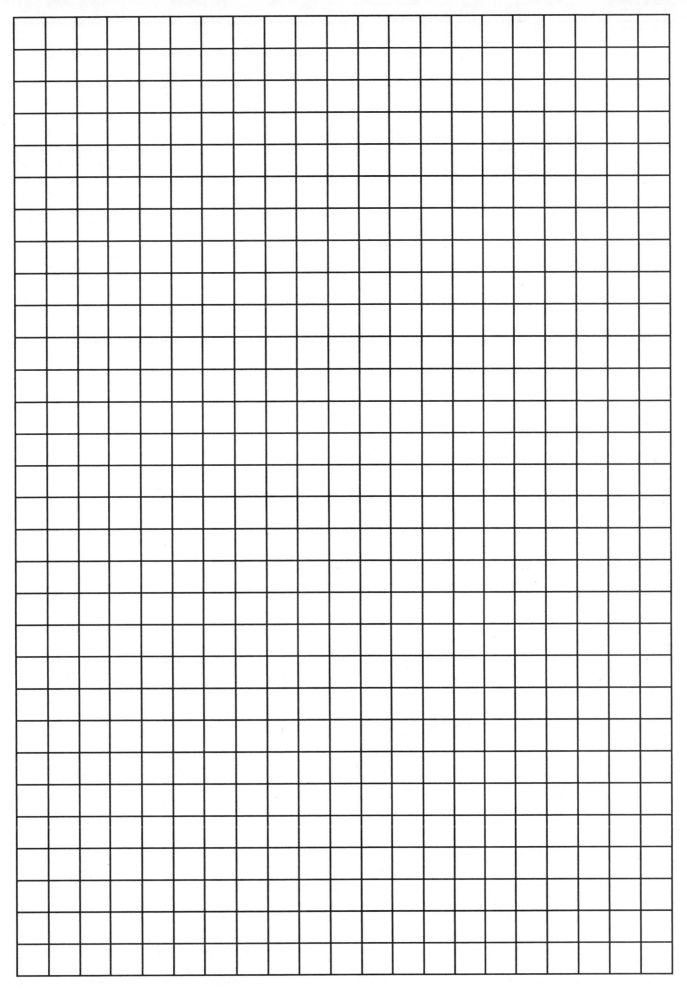

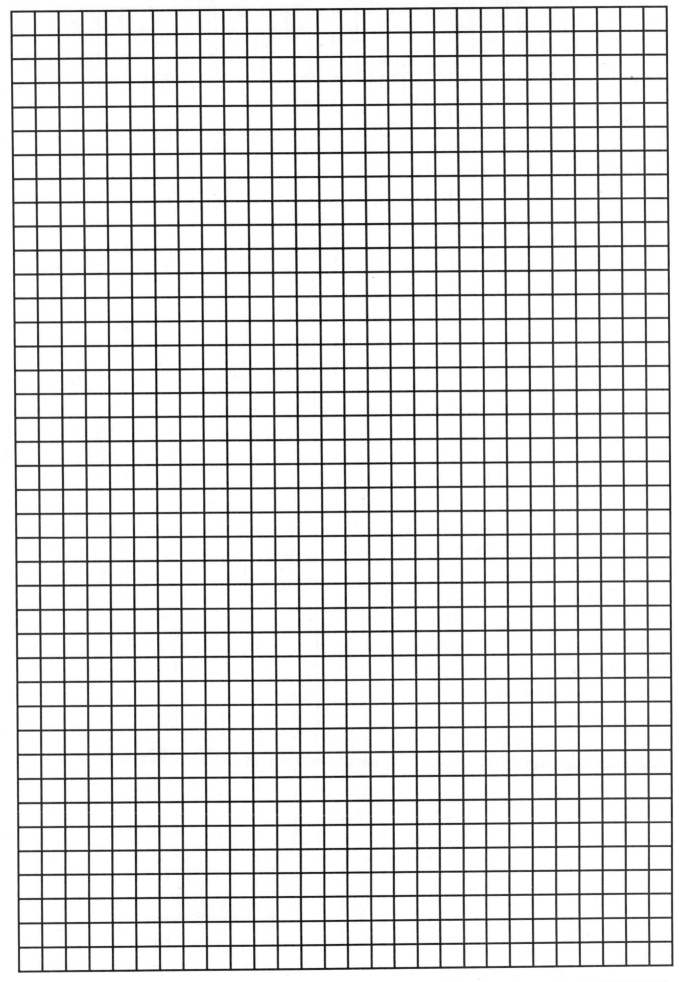

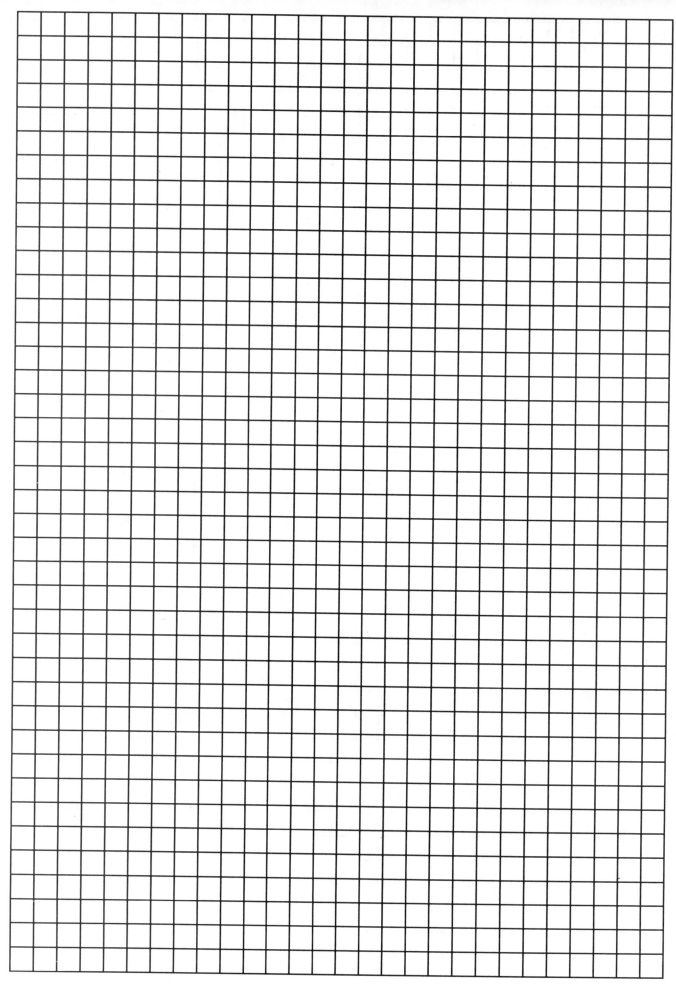

·

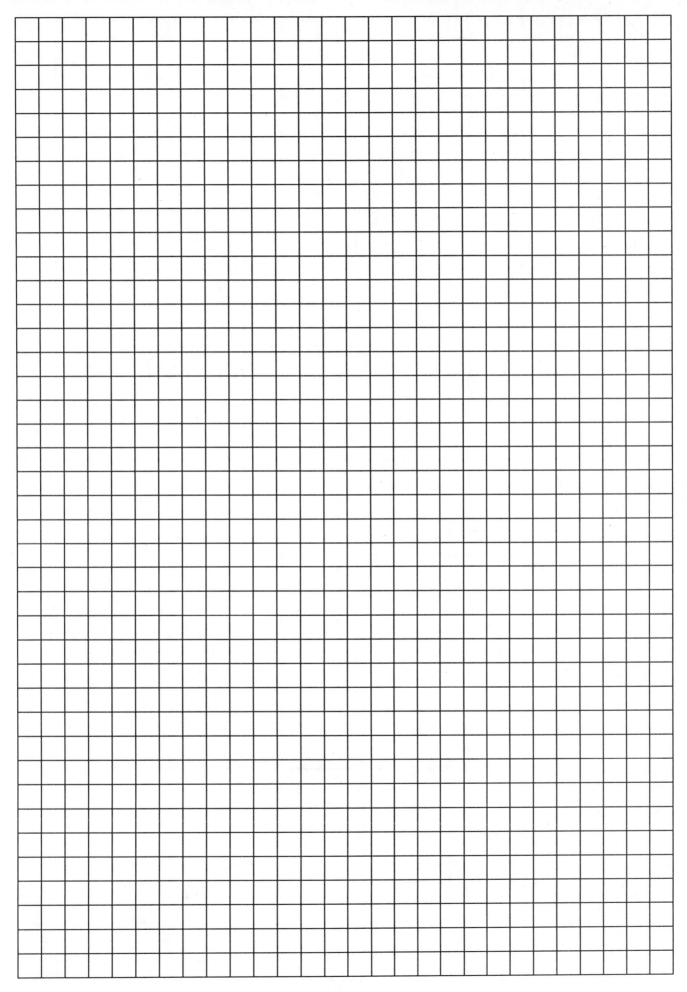

· GRAPH PAPER MASTERS **15**

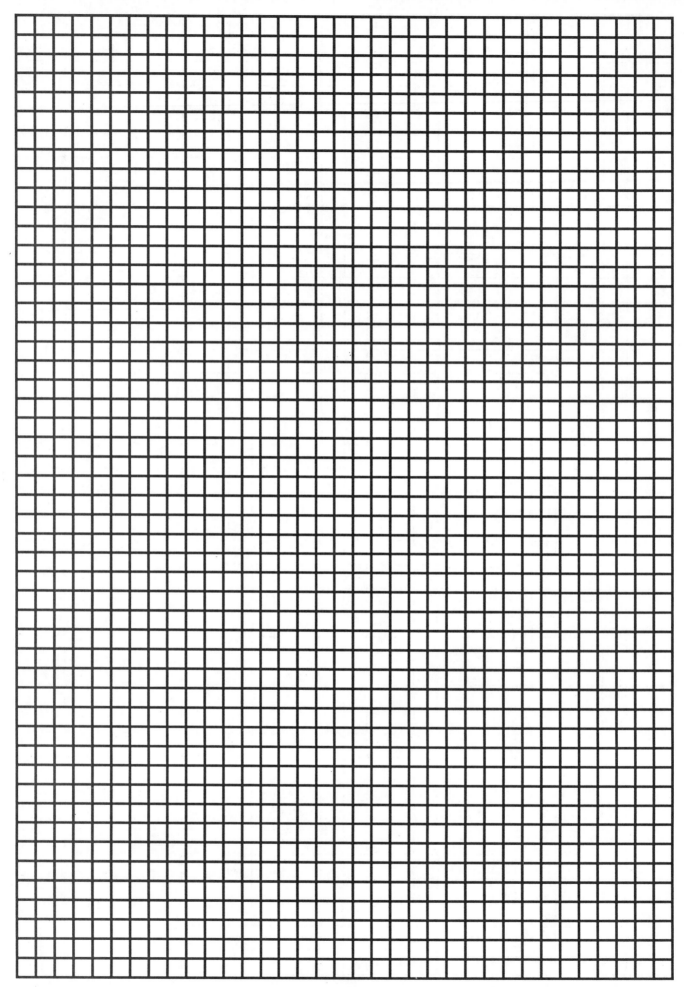

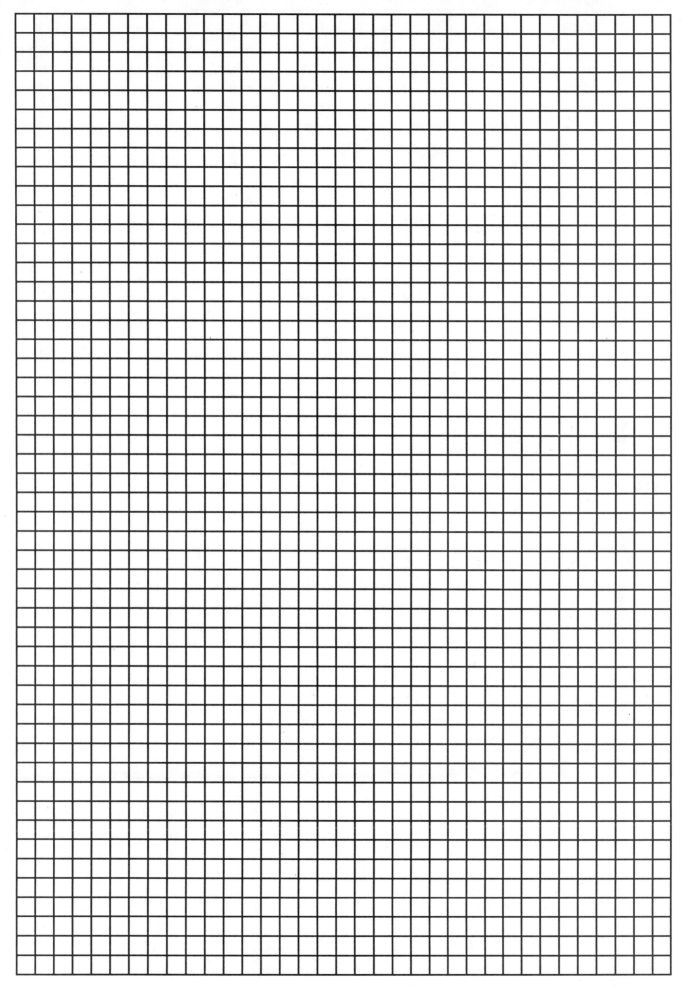

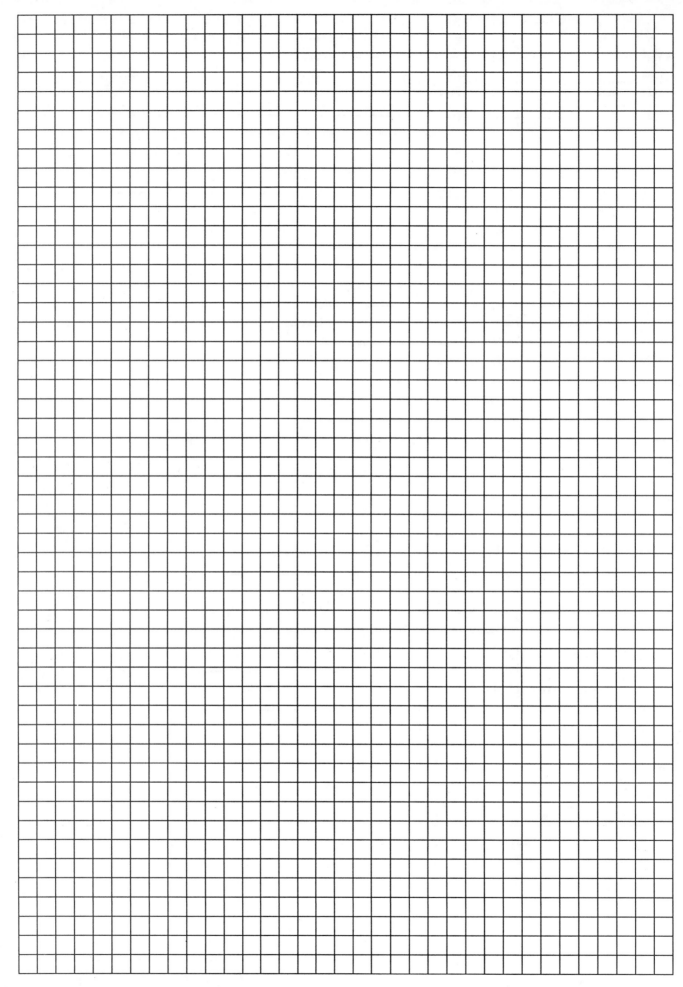

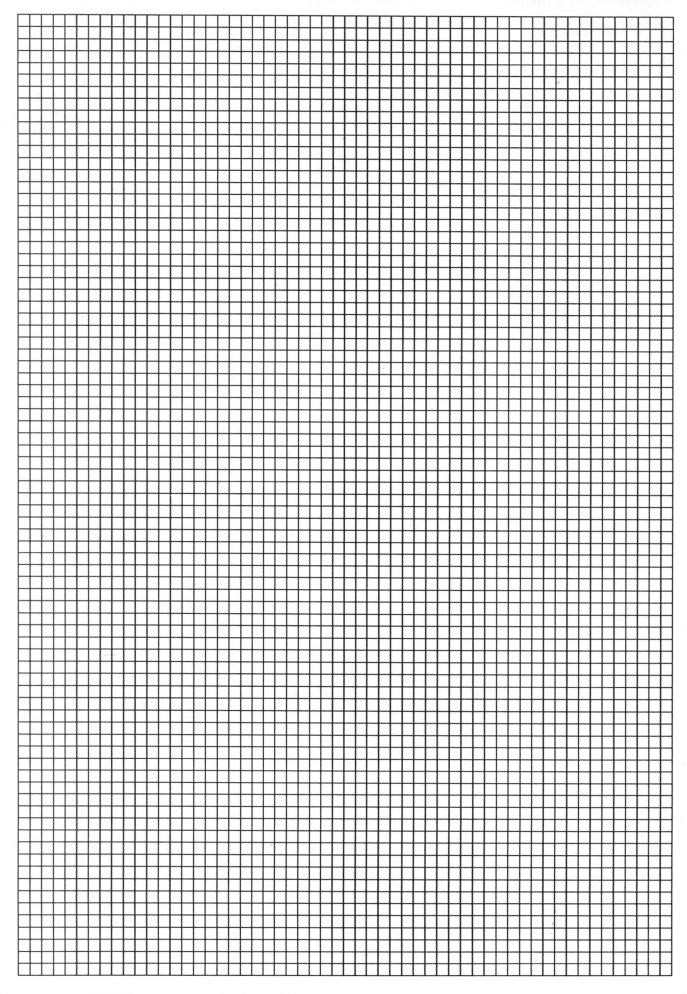

·

GRAPH PAPER MASTERS • Copyright © by Dale Seymour Publications

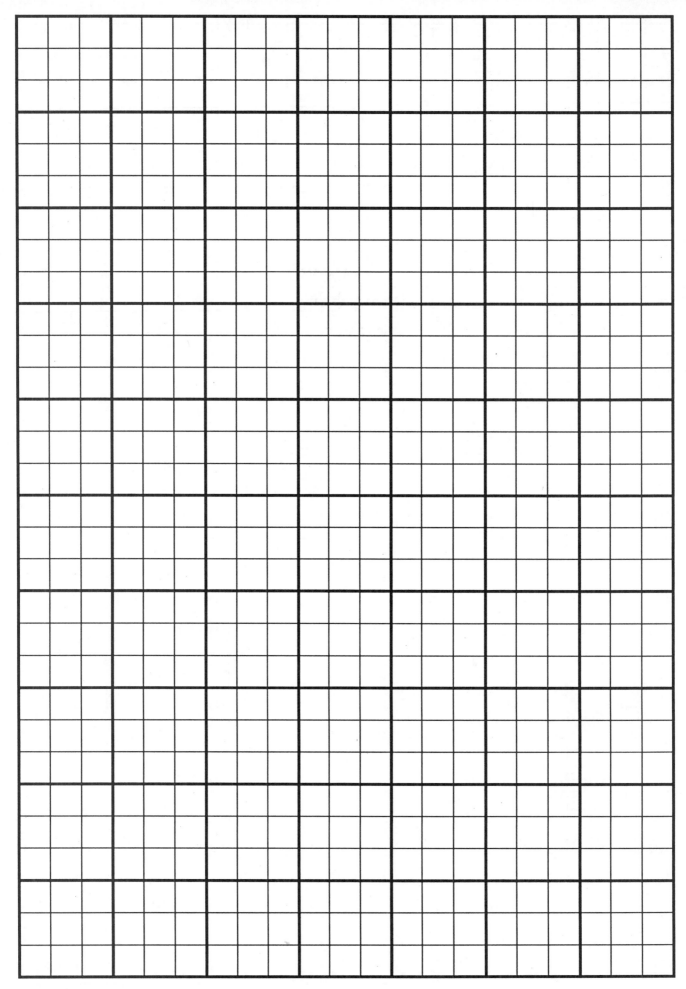

GRAPH PAPER MASTERS · Copyright © by Dale Seymour Publications

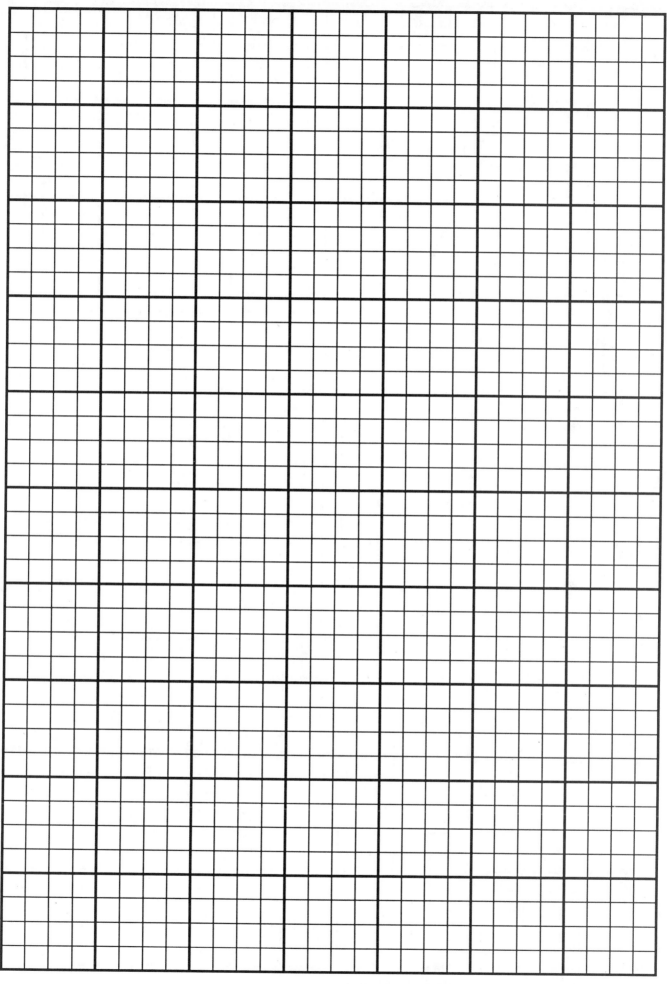

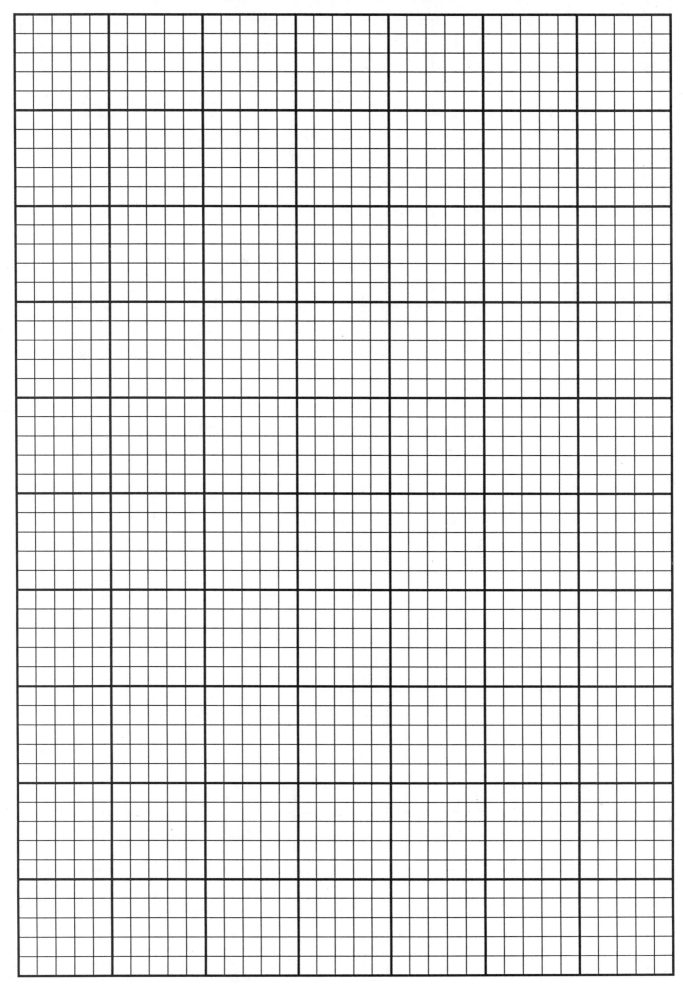

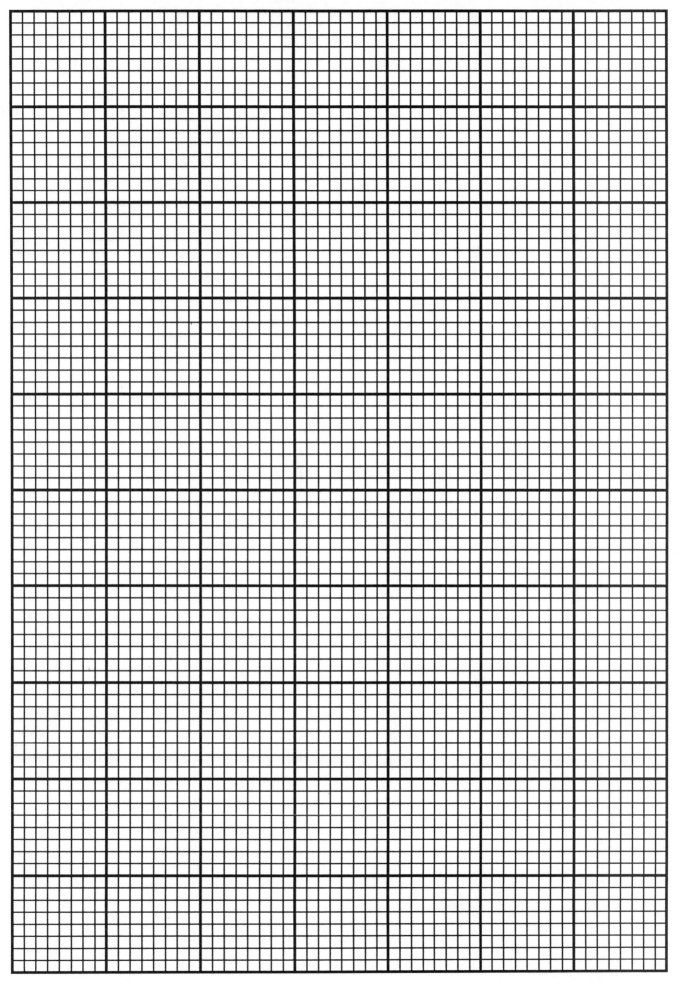

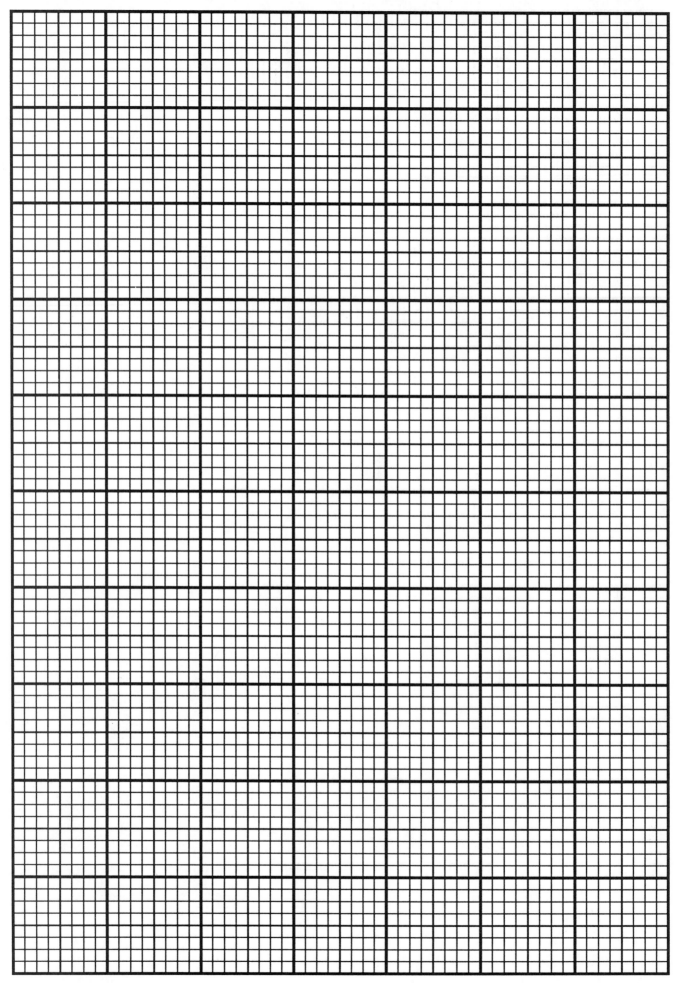

·

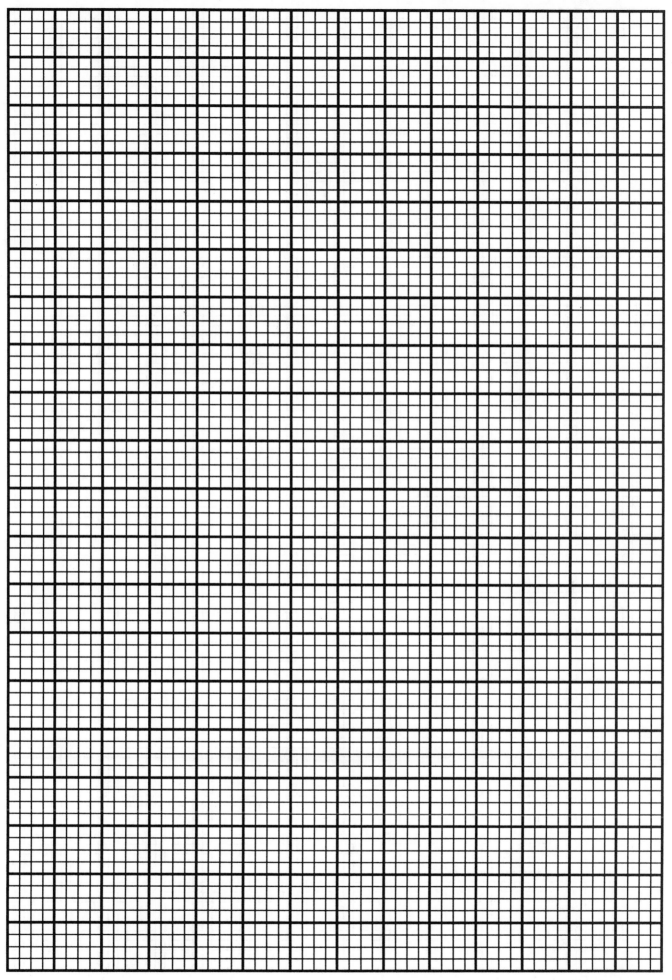

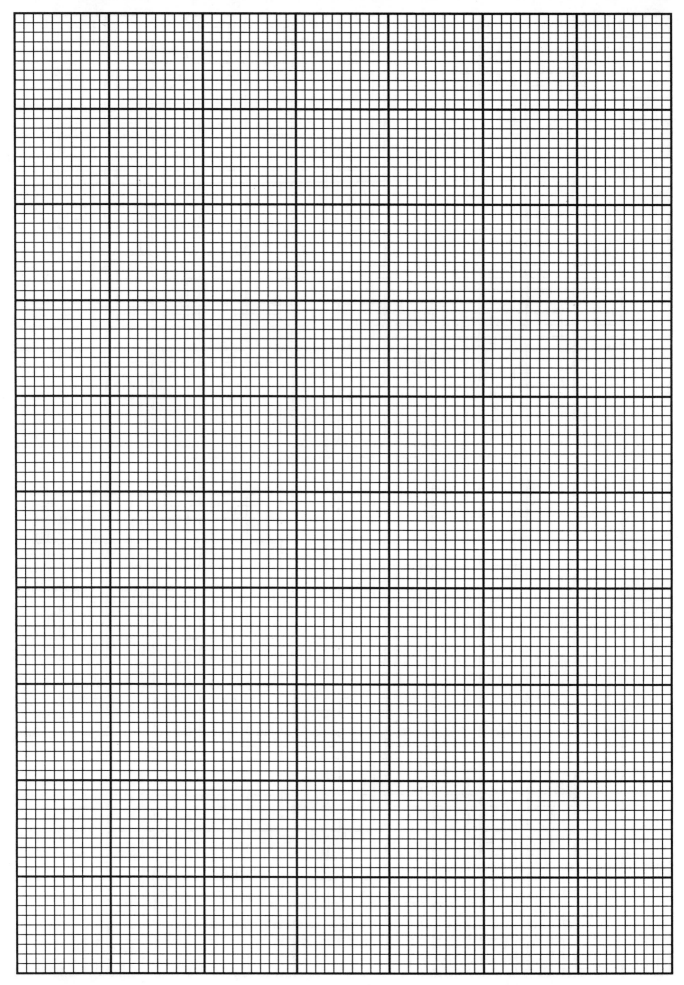

GRAPH PAPER MASTERS · Copyright © by Dale Seymour Publications

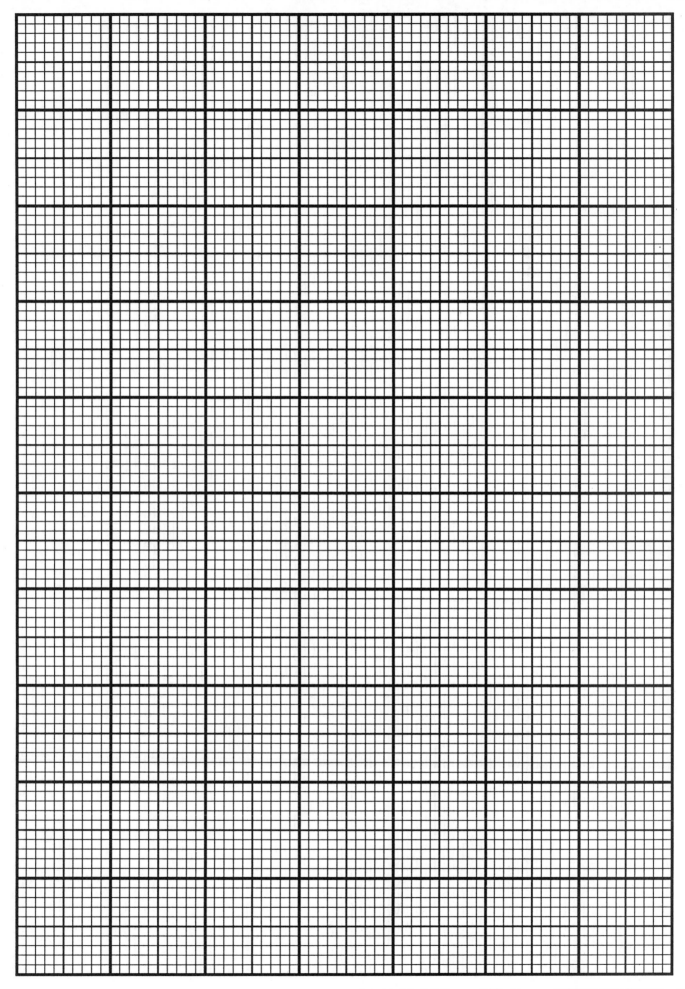

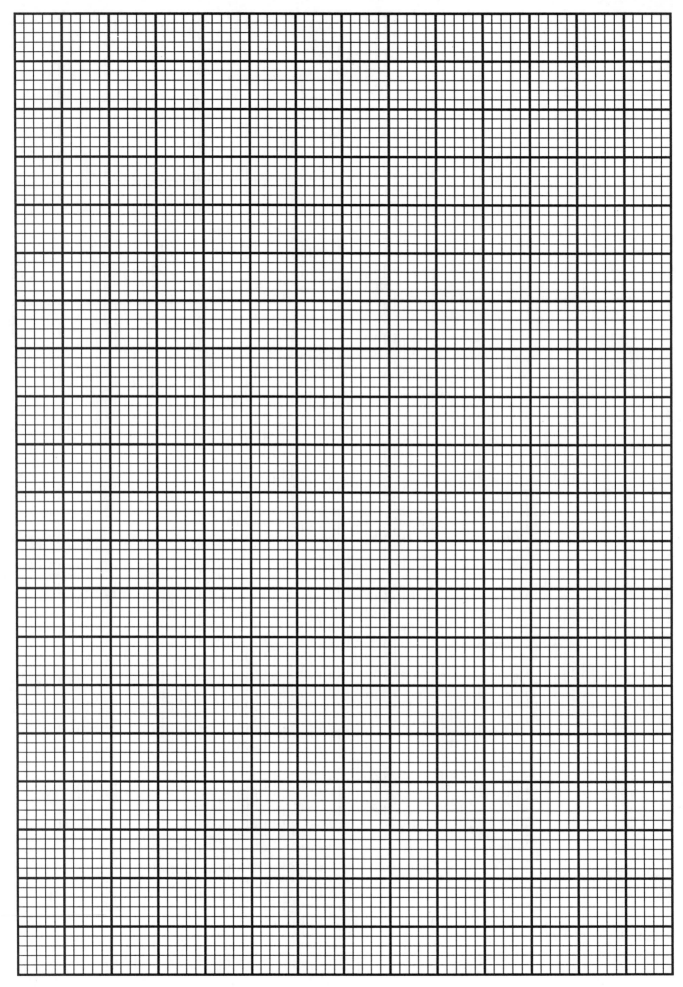

GRAPH PAPER MASTERS • Copyright © by Dale Seymour Publications

STANDARD MEASURE SKETCHING GRIDS

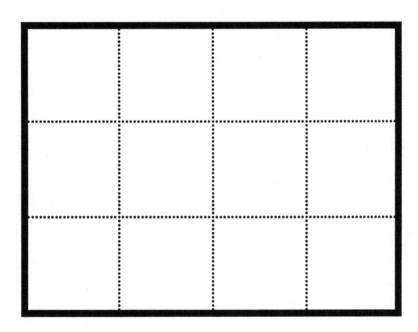

·

•

·

•

GRAPH PAPER MASTERS · Copyright © by Dale Seymour Publications

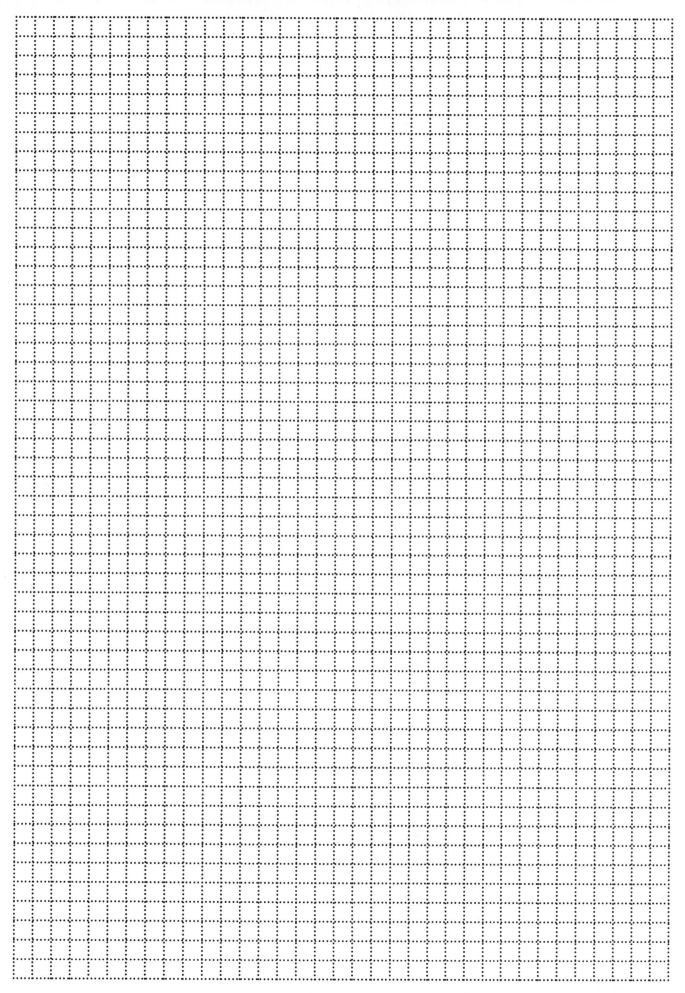

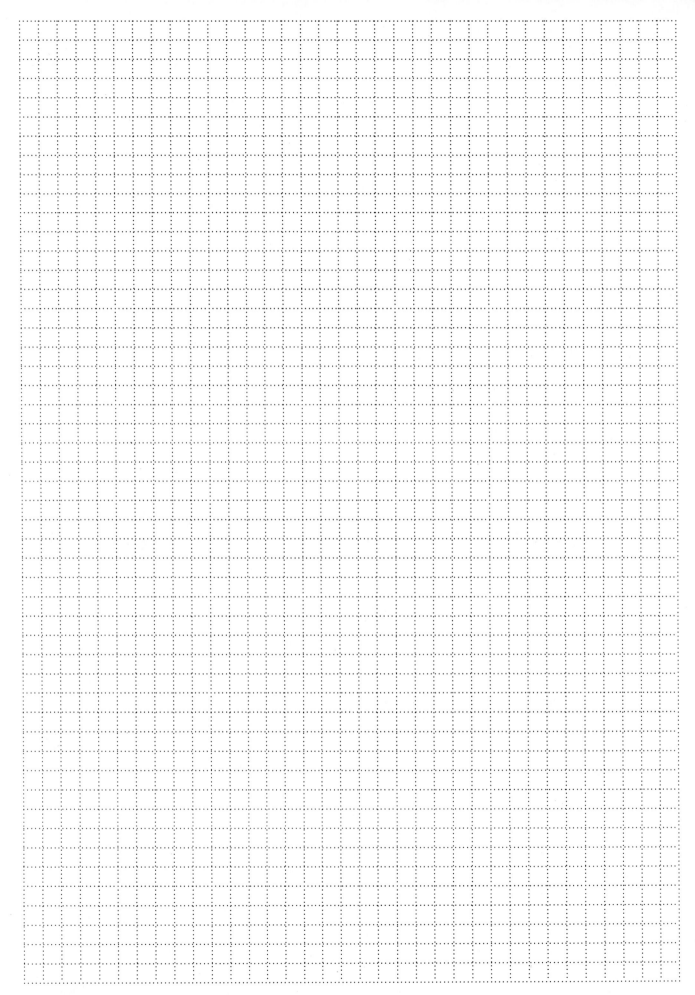

·

·

STANDARD
MEASURE
DOT PATTERNS

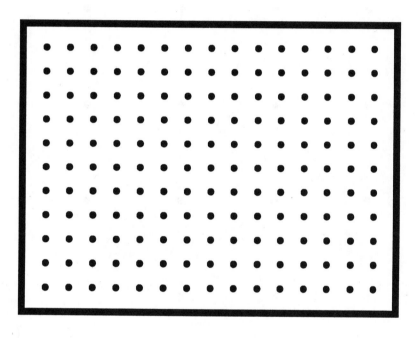

·

• GRAPH PAPER MASTERS **53**

·

· GRAPH PAPER MASTERS

·

· GRAPH PAPER MASTERS **59**

·

METRIC
MEASURE
GRIDS

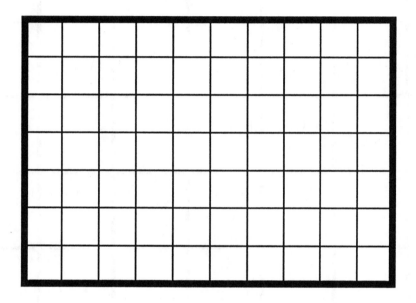

·

GRAPH PAPER MASTERS · Copyright © by Dale Seymour Publications

GRAPH PAPER MASTERS • Copyright © by Dale Seymour Publications

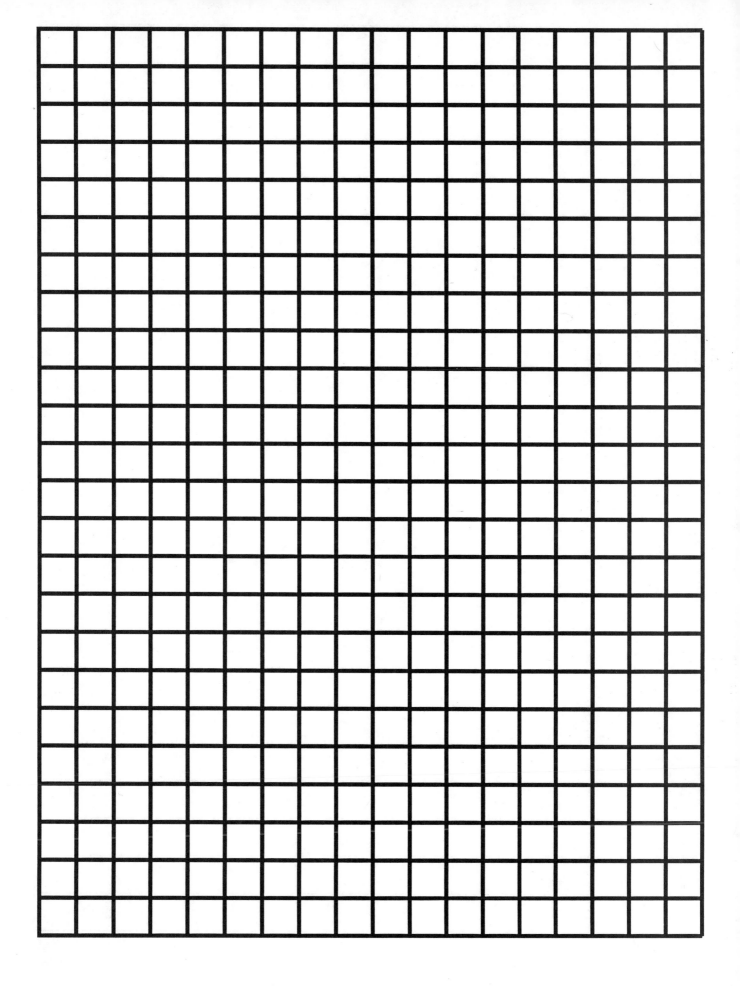

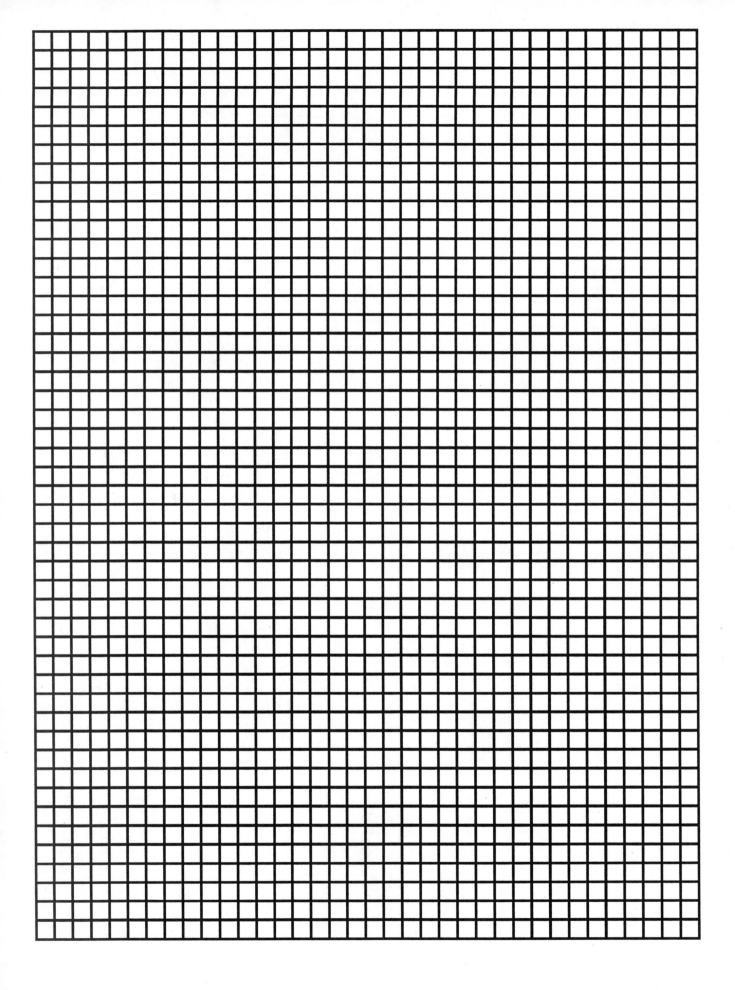

•

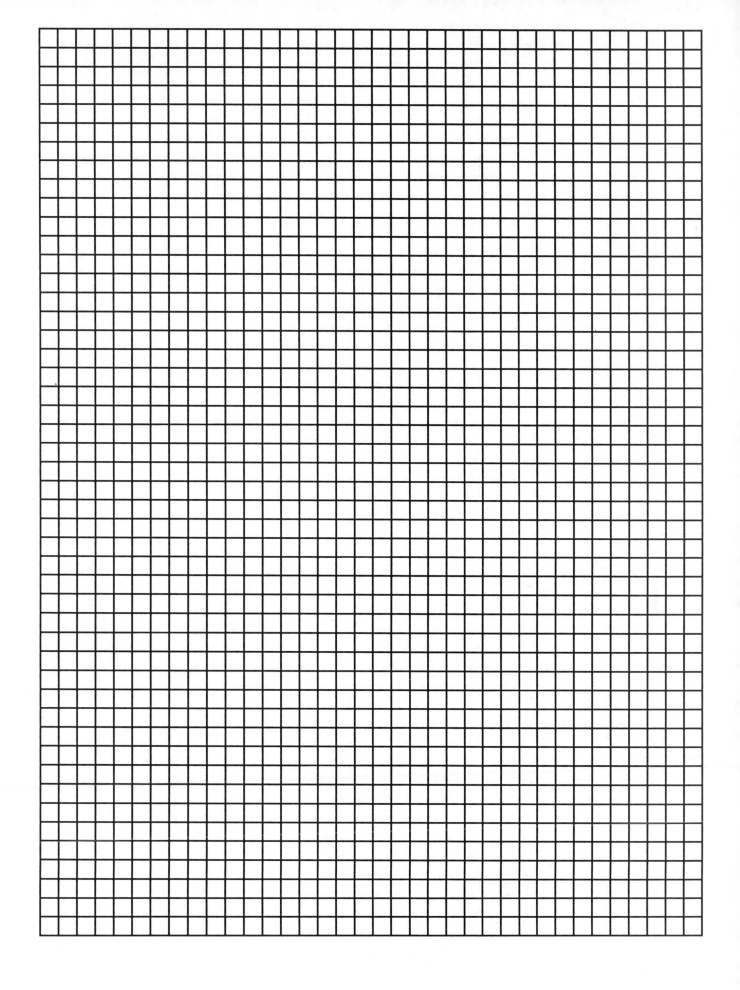

•

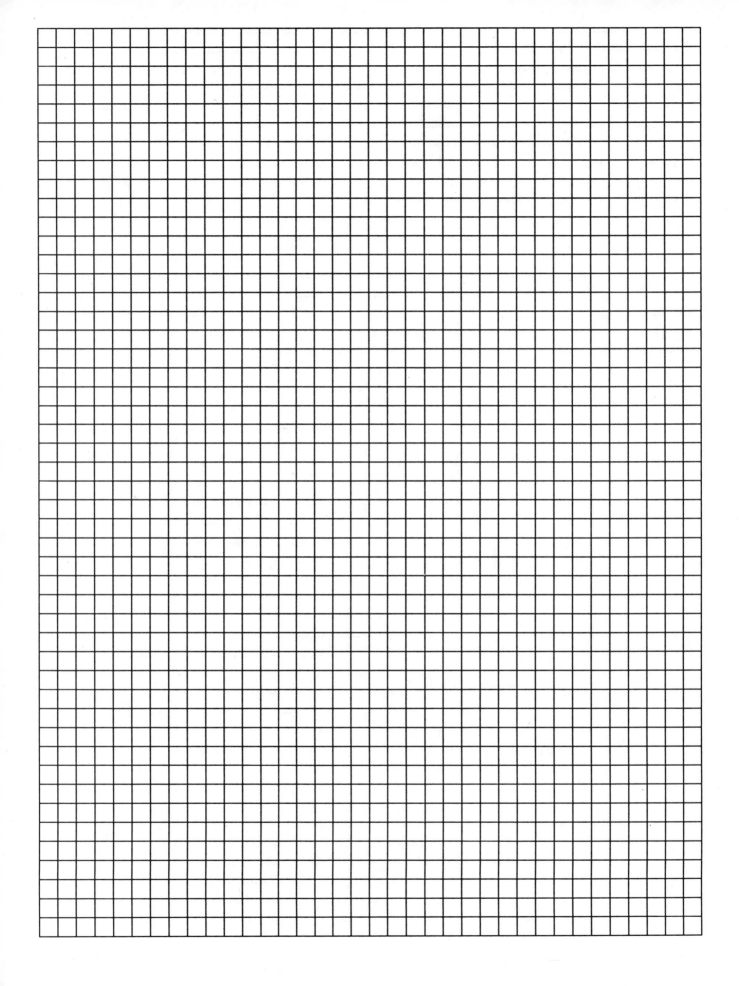

·

· Copyright © by Dale Seymour Publications

·

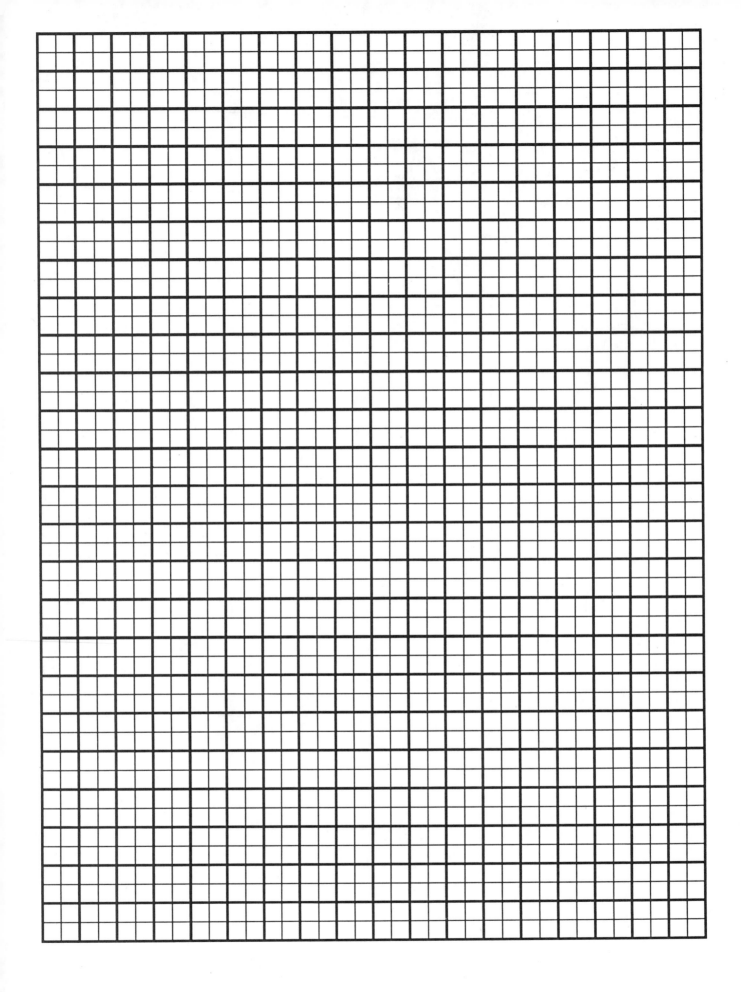

·

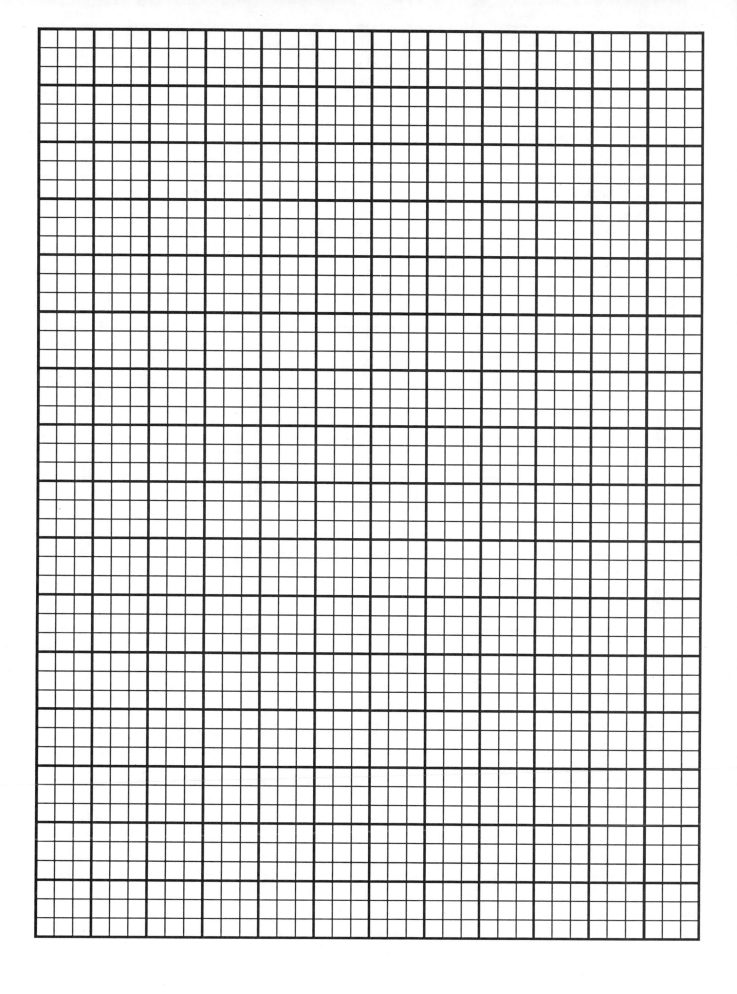

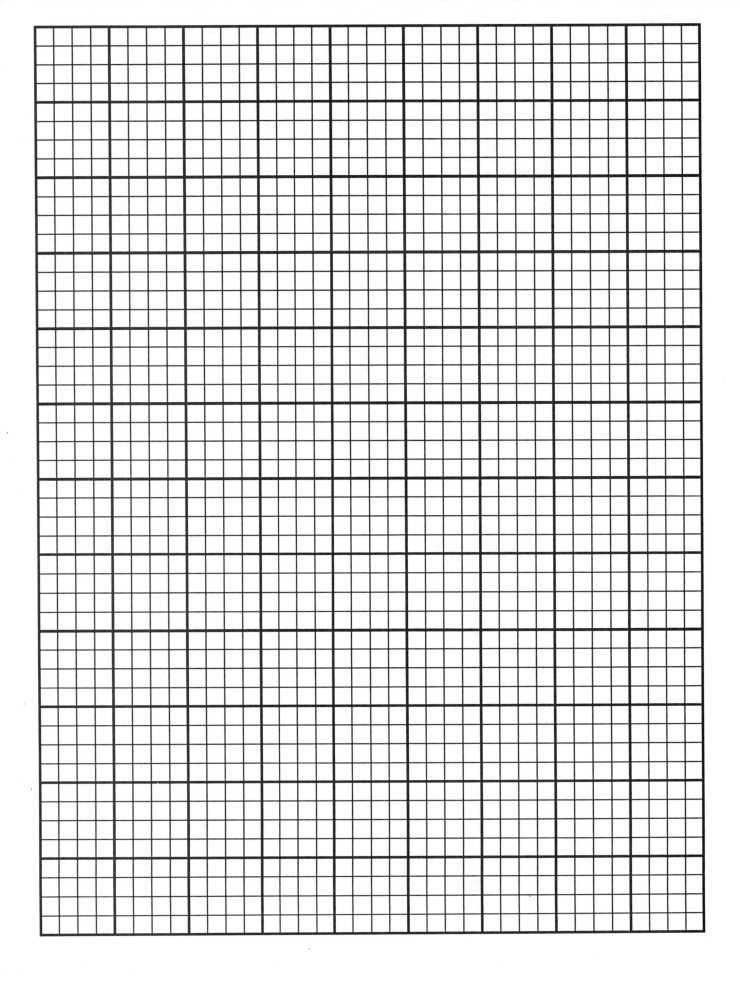

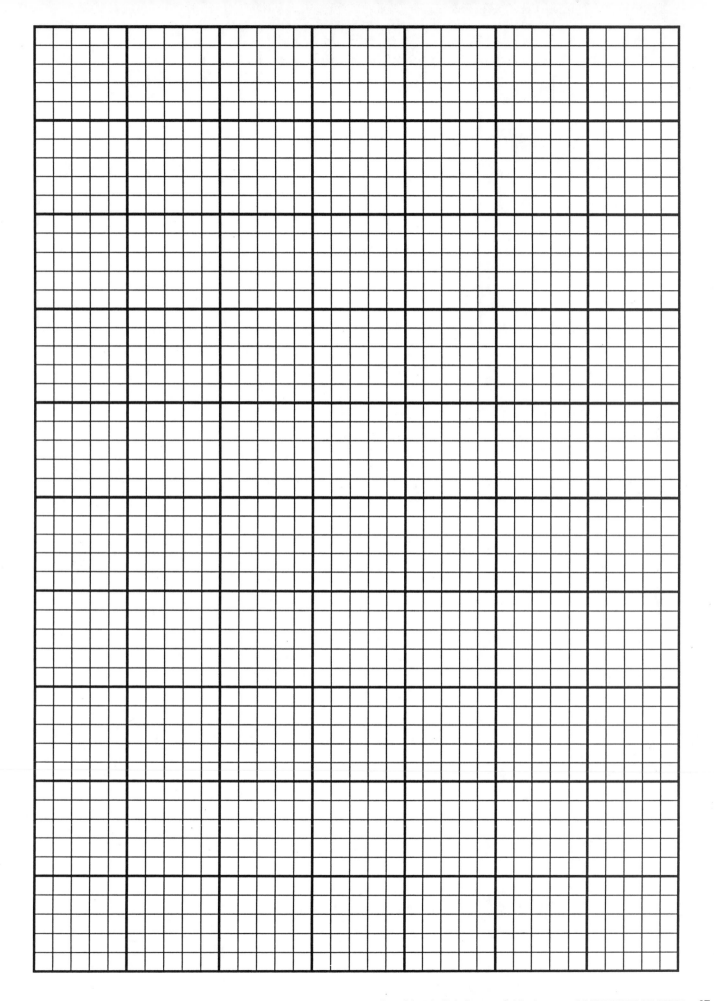

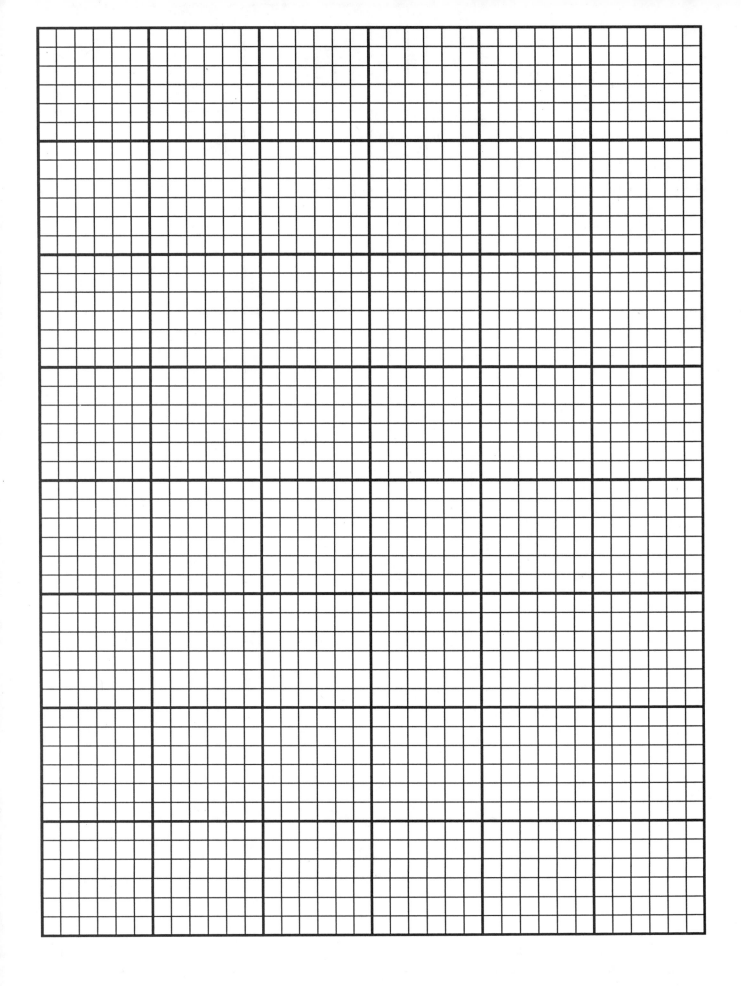

·

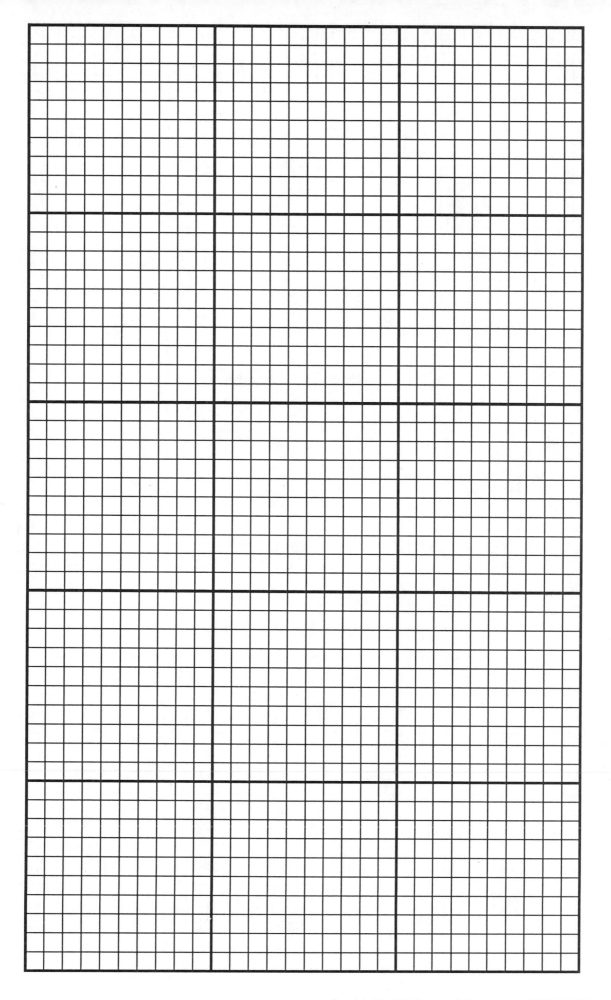

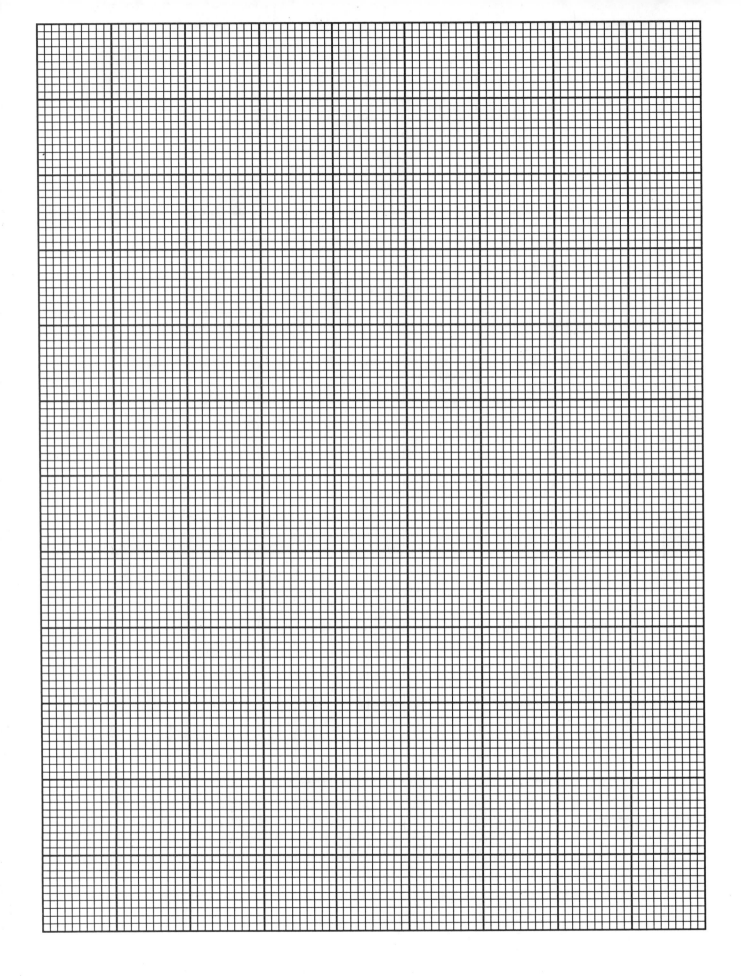

·

METRIC MEASURE SKETCHING GRIDS

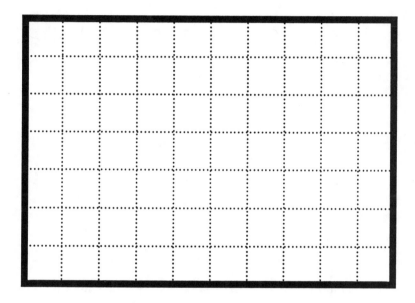

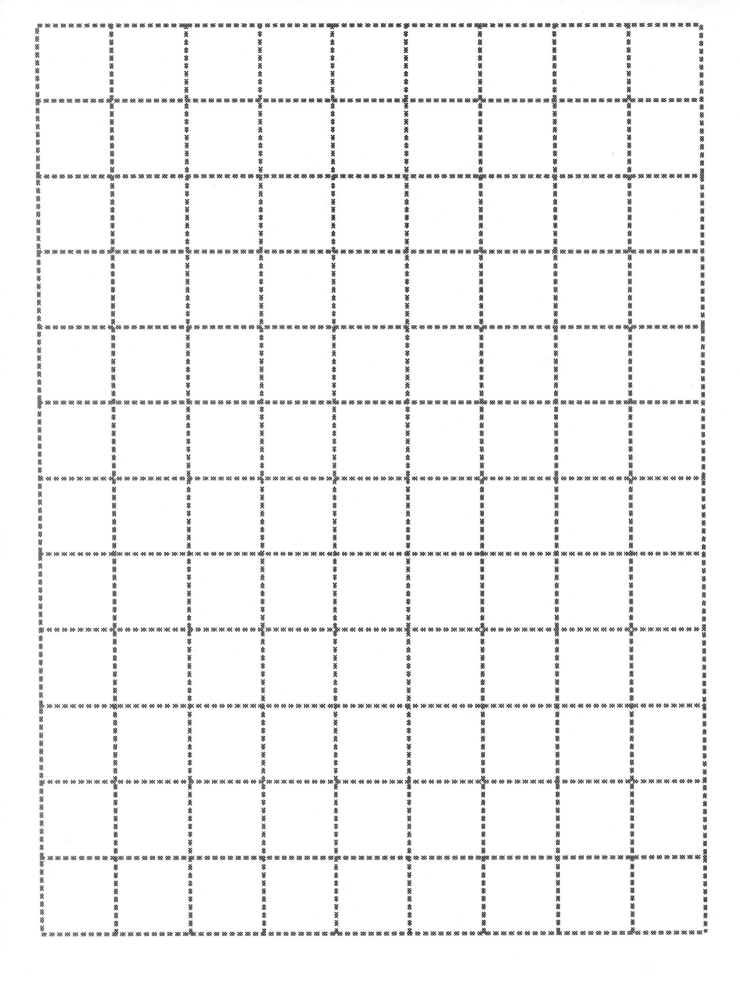

·

·

· Copyright © by Dale Seymour Publications

• GRAPH PAPER MASTERS **97**

GRAPH PAPER MASTERS • Copyright © by Dale Seymour Publications

• GRAPH PAPER MASTERS

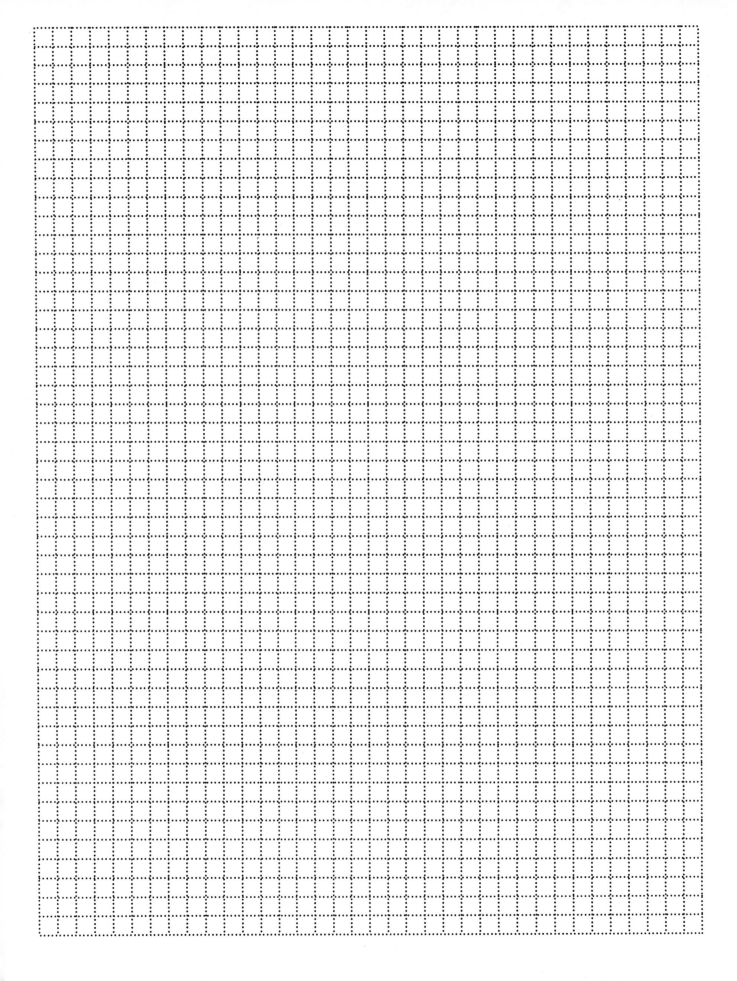

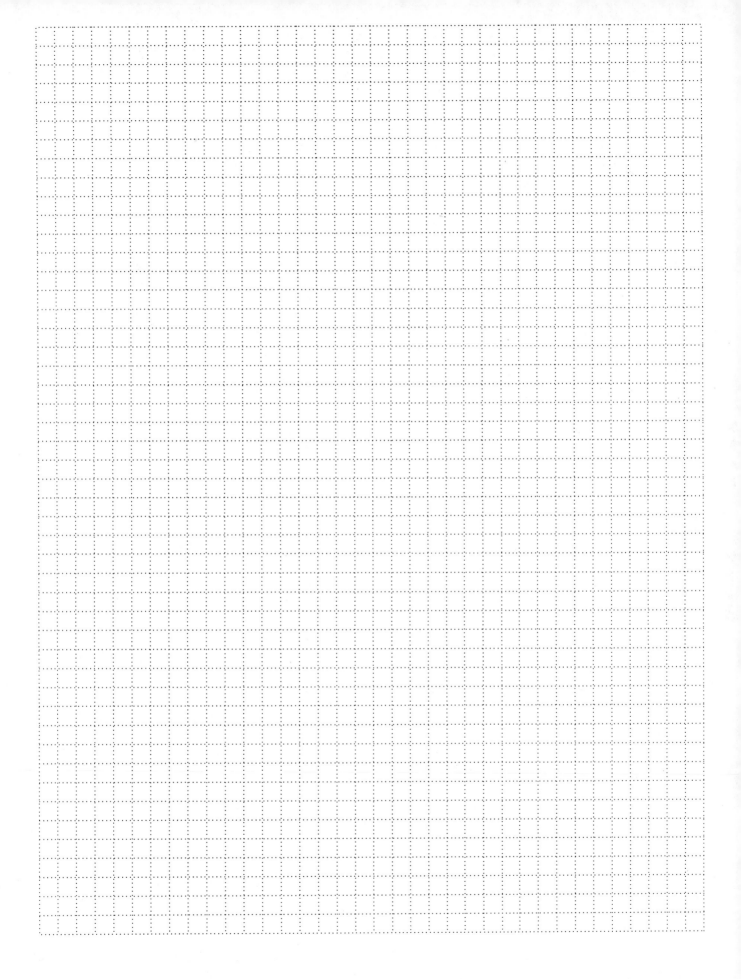

METRIC
MEASURE
DOT PATTERNS

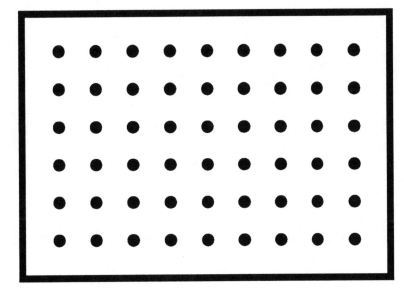

GRAPH PAPER MASTERS · Copyright © by Dale Seymour Publications

·

TRIANGULAR
GRIDS

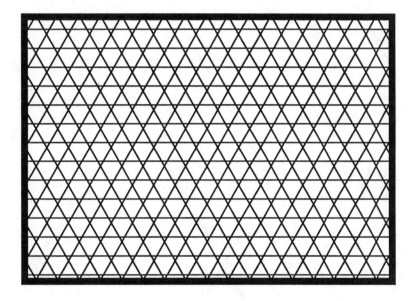

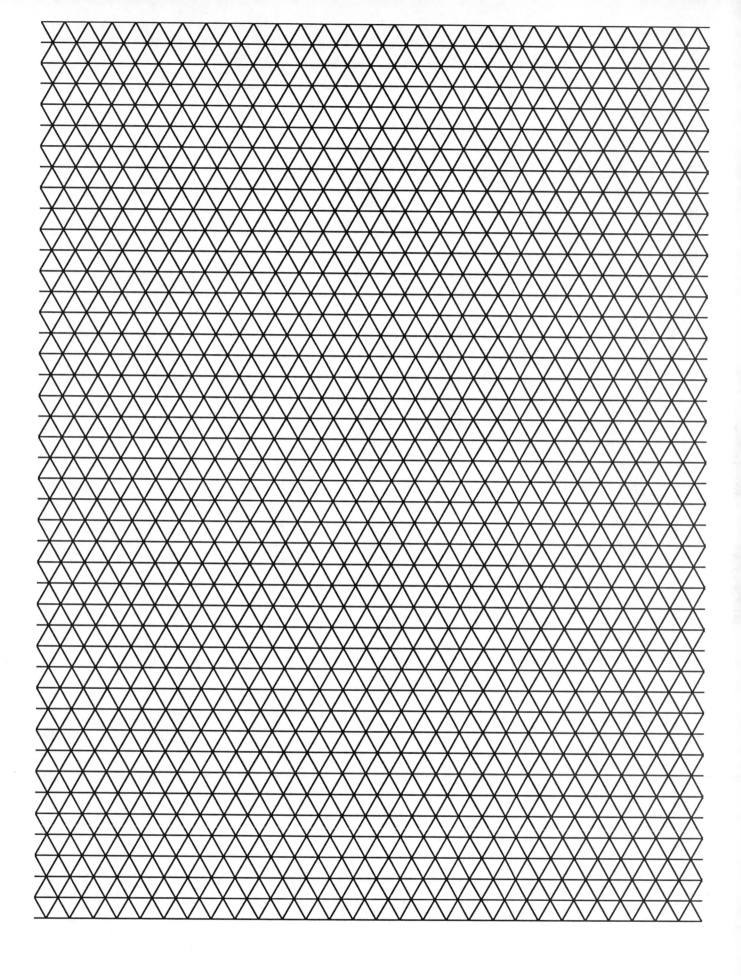

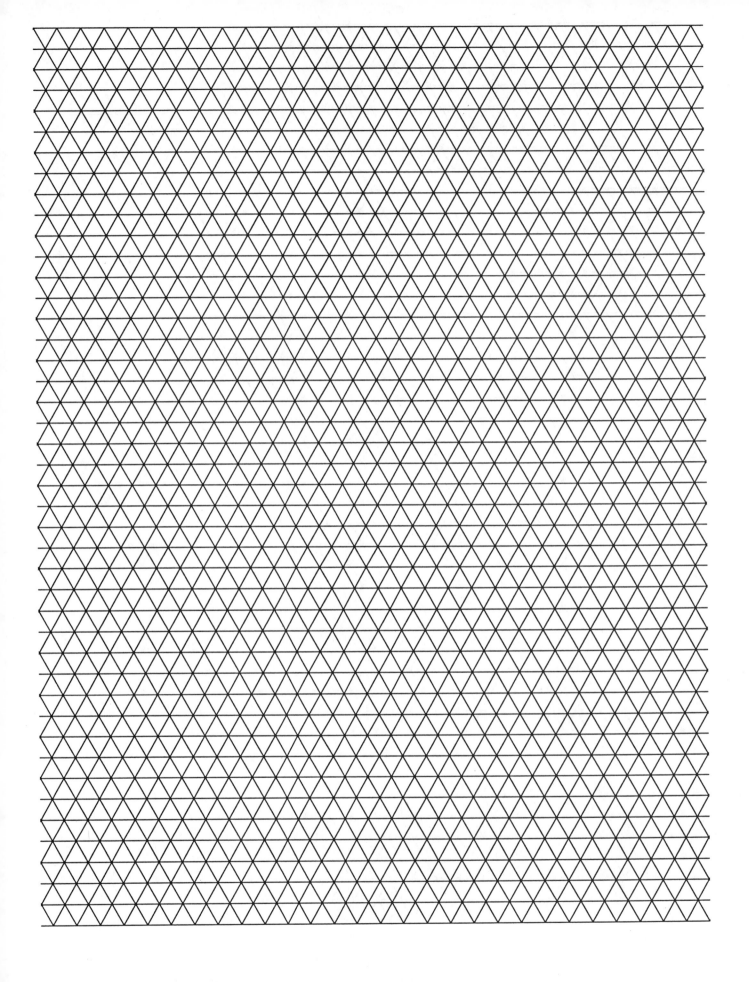

•

•

TRIANGULAR
SKETCHING
GRIDS

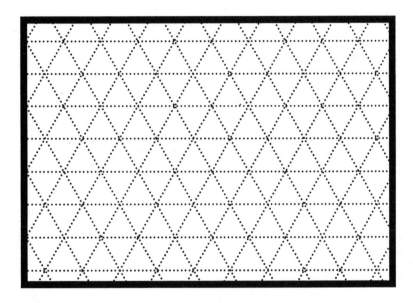

•

•

TRIANGULAR
DOT PATTERNS

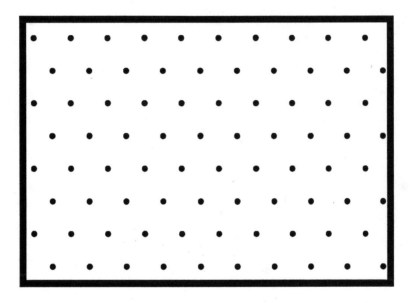

GRAPH PAPER MASTERS · Copyright © by Dale Seymour Publications

GRAPH PAPER MASTERS ·

HEXAGONAL GRIDS

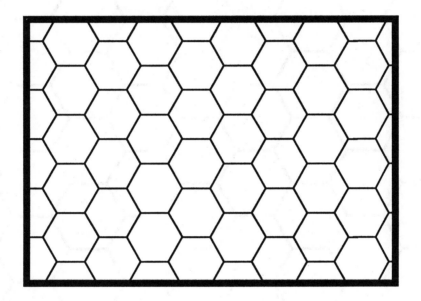

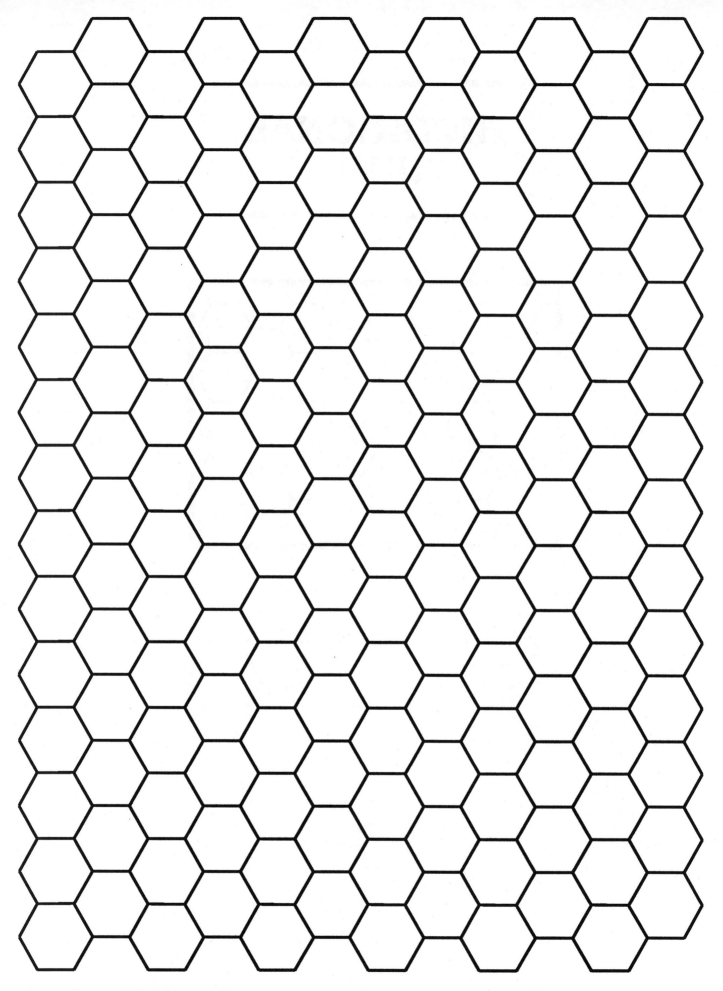

•

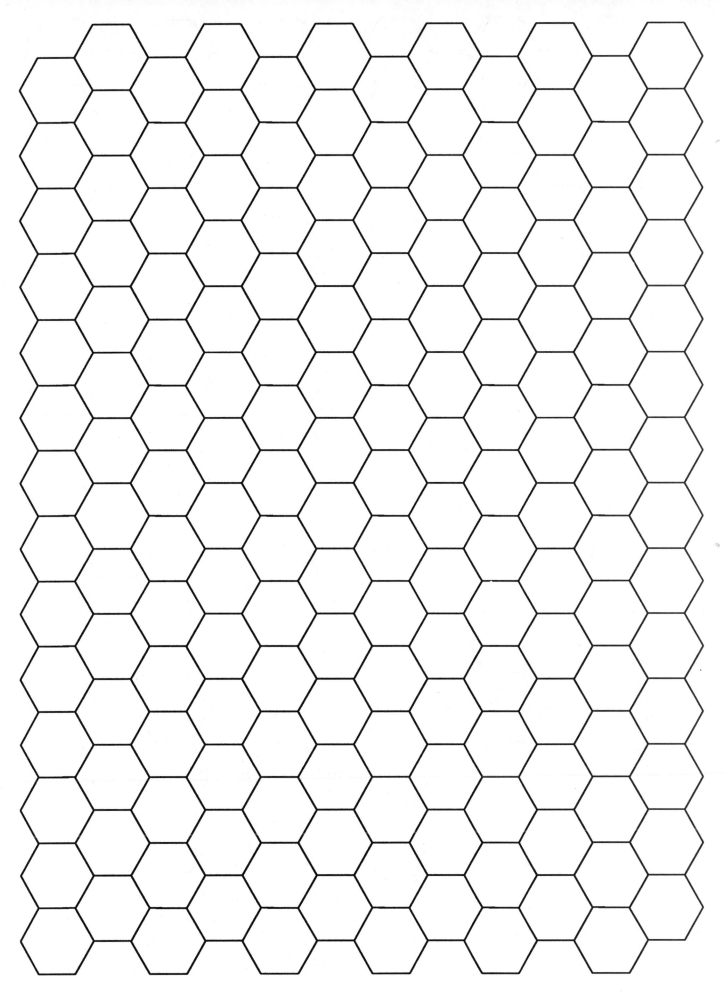

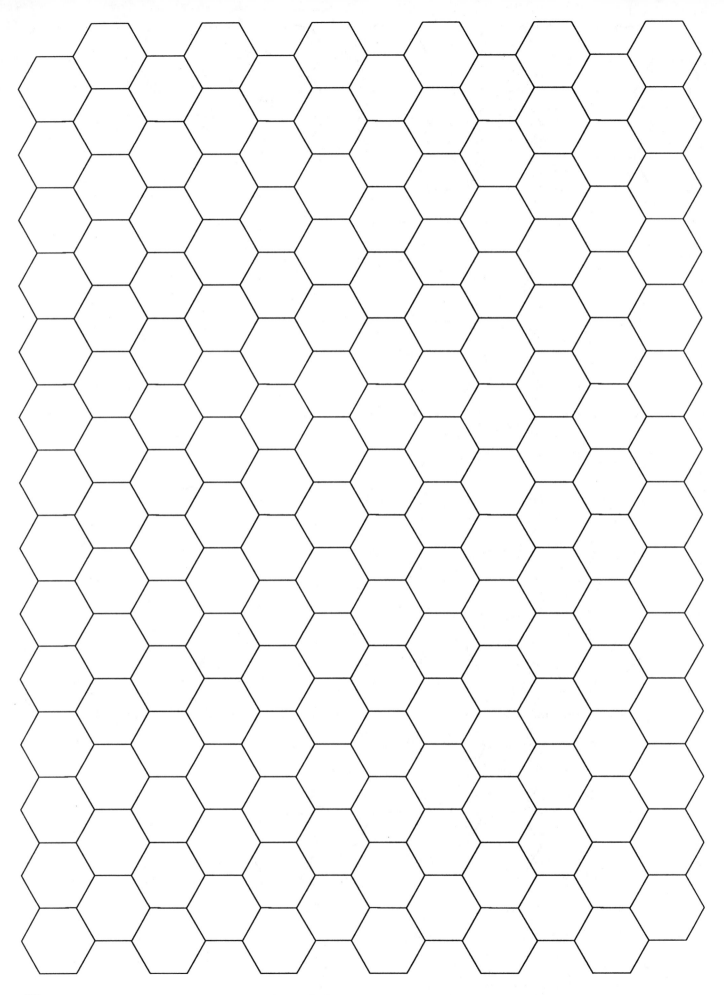

GRAPH PAPER MASTERS •

HEXAGONAL SKETCHING GRIDS

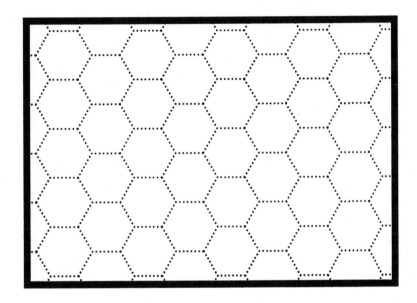

• GRAPH PAPER MASTERS **161**

•

•

HEXAGONAL
DOT PATTERNS

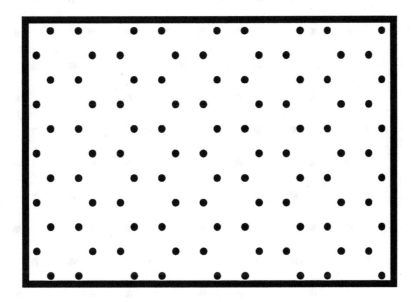

GRAPH PAPER MASTERS · Copyright © by Dale Seymour Publications

·

·

POLAR
COORDINATE
GRIDS

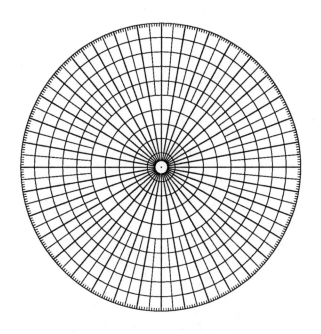

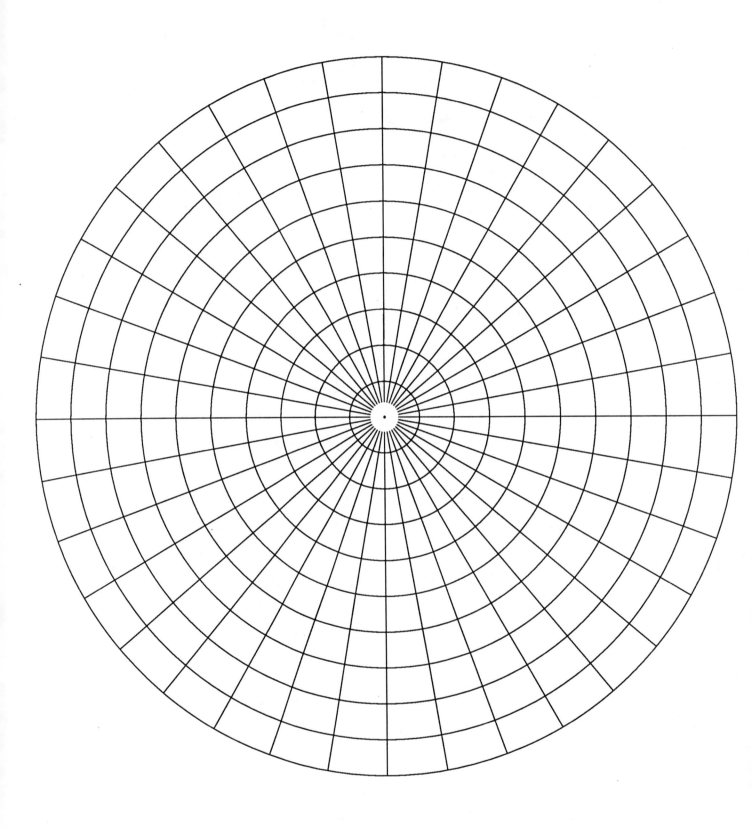

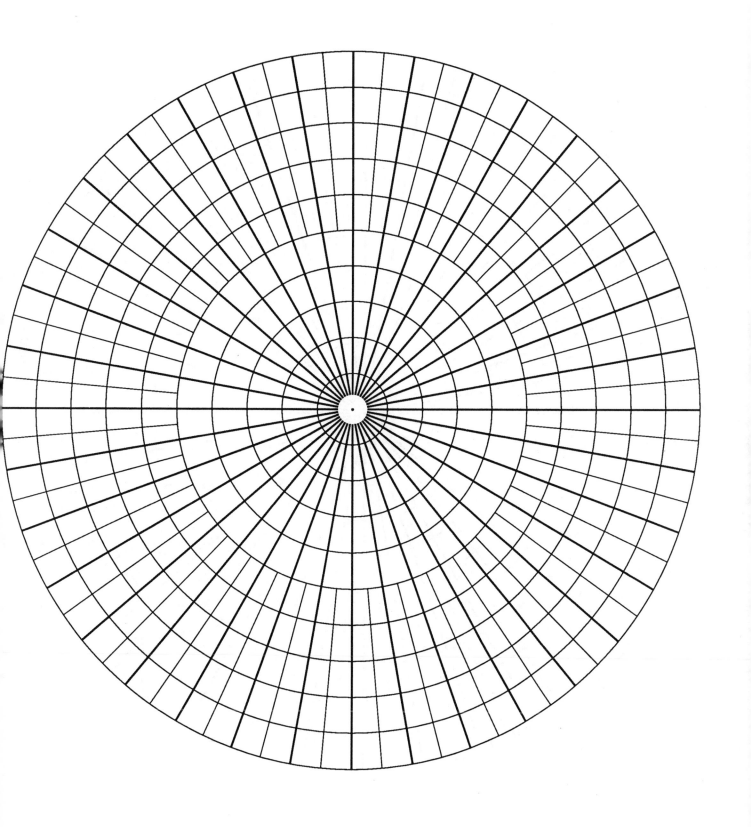

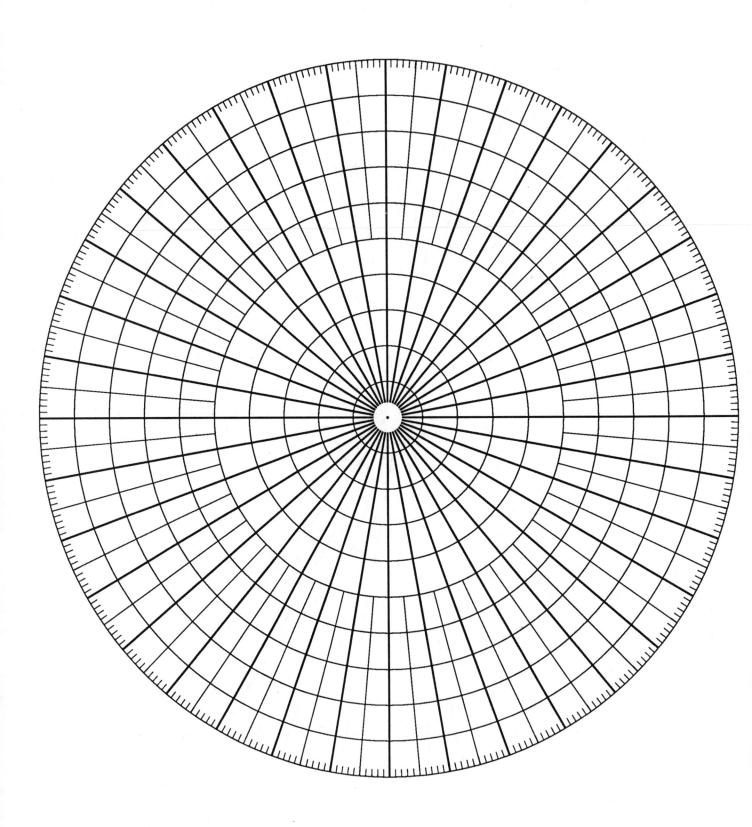